THE POPE IN IRELAND
A PICTORIAL RECORD

GILL & MACMILLAN

FOREWORD

'Like St Patrick, I too have heard "the voice of the Irish" calling to me, and so I have come to you, to all of you in Ireland.'

With this reference to the country's ancient Christian tradition, Pope John Paul II began his homily to a massive congregation assembled in Dublin's Phoenix Park. One and a quarter million people – the largest crowd ever seen in Ireland – had come to hear the Pope celebrate Mass at the start of an historic pastoral visit.

The Pope in Ireland: a pictorial record is a permanent memento of John Paul II's three-day pilgrimage. It recaptures the atmosphere of joy and faith during those unforgettable days from 29 September to 1 October 1979.

The book recalls the Pope's solemn urging in Dublin for spiritual renewal of modern lifestyles, his anguished and passionate plea at Drogheda for peace and forgiveness in Northern Ireland, the uninhibited enthusiasm of his young audience at Galway, his tenderness towards the sick at Knock and his strong reaffirmation of the ideal of the Christian family at Limerick. Two and a half million people saw Pope John Paul II during his pilgrimage in Ireland. Many millions more heard his resounding message on television and radio. All were affected deeply by his words and by his warm personality. For them this book is a reminder of a unique experience which will be treasured for a lifetime.

In the Aer Lingus Jumbo *St Patrick* which brought him from Rome to Dublin on Saturday 29 September 1979, the Pope told the journalists who travelled with him:
'I am going to Ireland to pray.'

The Irish bishops declared in a pastoral letter read in churches throughout the country before the Pope's visit:
'News of the coming visit of Pope John Paul II brings immense rejoicing to the hearts of all Irish people. It is with eager anticipation that we now prepare to give an historic welcome to the first Pope in history to visit this island ... The Pope has said that he is coming to Ireland for a pastoral visit. The desire of a pastor is to meet and to know and to talk with his people. We know that hundreds of thousands of Irish people will respond to his invitation.'

Several days before his departure the Pope told a crowd in St Peter's Square:

'Today my heart is already in Ireland which is so profoundly linked with the Catholic Church... I want to express my indestructible confidence that my visit will serve the great cause of peace and reconciliation which is so much desired by the entire Irish nation.'

'NÁRA TURAS É IN AISTEAR GURA LEAS DÚINN GACH ORLACH'
'MAY THE JOURNEY BE NOT IN VAIN MAY WE BENEFIT BY EVERY INCH'
(Modern translation by Seán O Ríordáin of a religious verse from a fifteenth century manuscript).

St Patrick

6

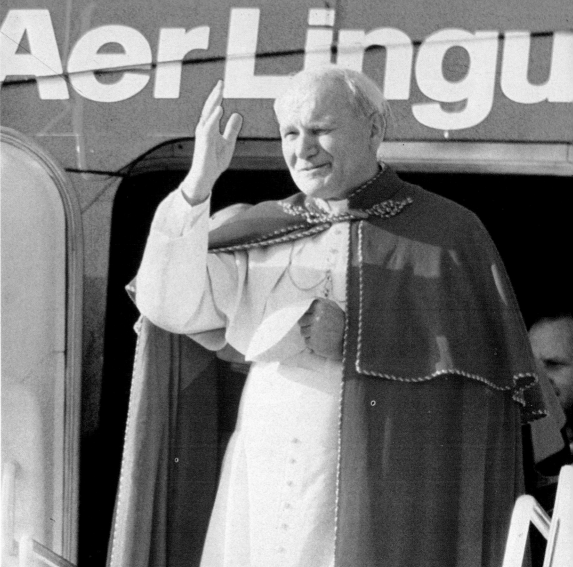

In brilliant sunshine, a Pope, for the first time ever, prepares to set foot on Irish soil.

Ireland Welcomes Pope John Paul II

Before inspecting the guard of honour, the Pope is welcomed by an enthusiastic crowd and, in a characteristic gesture, kisses the ground.

In his speech of welcome, Cardinal Tonas O Fiaich, Archbishop of Armagh, told the Pope: 'You come as a messenger of peace to a troubled land.'

President Hillery declared: 'A long-cherished hope of our people has been fulfilled in your coming.'

'I am grateful to my brothers in the episcopate who are here to greet me in the name of the whole Church in Ireland that I love so much. I am very happy to walk among you – in the footsteps of Saint Patrick and in the path of the gospel that he left you as a great heritage – being convinced that Christ is here: "Christ before me, Christ behind me, Christ in the heart of every man who thinks of me, Christ in the mouth of every man who speaks of me".'

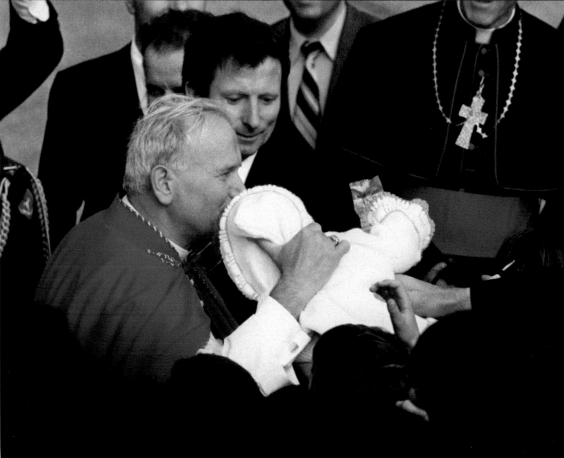

'At this moment of my arrival I feel the need to express my esteem for the Christian traditions of this land, as well as the gratitude of the Catholic Church for the glorious contribution made by Ireland over the centuries to the spreading of the faith. From this capital city I send my greetings to all the Irish throughout the world.'

As the Pope is welcomed at Dublin Airport, vast crowds *overleaf,* await him in the nearby Phoenix Park.

'Dear brothers and sisters in Jesus Christ, like Saint Patrick, I too have heard "the voice of the Irish" calling to me, and so I have come to you, to all of you in Ireland...You Irish Catholics have kept and loved the unity and peace of the Catholic Church, treasuring it above all earthly treasure. Your people have spread this love for the Catholic Church everywhere they went, in every century of your history. This has been done by the earliest monks and the missionaries of Europe's Dark Ages, by the refugees from persecution, by the exiles and by the missionaries – men and women – of the last century and this one.'

'We are one in faith and spirit with the vast throng which filled this Phoenix Park on the occasion of the last great Eucharist hosting held on this spot, at the Eucharistic Congress in 1932.'

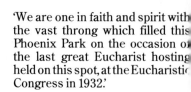

23

'On Sunday mornings in Ireland, no one seeing the great crowds making their way to and from Mass could have any doubt about Ireland's devotion to the Mass. For them a whole Catholic people is seen to be faithful to the Lord's command: "Do this in memory of Me."'

'As I stand here, in the company of so many hundreds of thousands of Irish men and women, I am thinking of how many times across how many centuries, the Eucharist has been celebrated in this land. How many and how varied the places where Mass has been offered – in stately mediaeval and in splendid modern cathedrals; in early monastic and in modern churches; at Mass rocks in the glens and forests by "hunted priests" and in poor thatch-covered chapels, for a people poor in worldly goods but rich in the things of the spirit, in "wake-houses" or "station houses", or at great open-air hostings of the faithful – on the top of Croagh Patrick and at Lough Derg. Small matter where the Mass was offered, for the Irish, it was always the Mass that mattered. How many have found in it the spiritual strength to live, even through the times of greatest hardship and poverty, through days of perse-cution and vexations.'

'Pervading materialism imposes its dominion on man today in many different forms and with an aggressiveness that spares no one. The most sacred principles, which were the sure guides for the behaviour of individuals and society, are being hollowed-out by false pretences concerning freedom, the sacredness of life, the indissolubility of marriage, the true sense of human sexuality, the right attitude towards the material goods that progress has to offer.

Many people now are tempted to self-indulgence and consumer-ism, and human identity is often defined by what one owns. Prosperity and affluence, even when they are only beginning to be available to larger strata of society, tend to make people assume that they have a right to all that pros-perity can bring, and thus they can become more selfish in their demands. Everybody wants a full freedom in all the areas of human behaviour and new models of morality are being proposed in the name of would-be freedom.'

'When the moral fibre of a nation is weakened, when the sense of personal responsibility is diminished, then the door is open for the justification of injustices, for violence in all its forms, and for the manipulation of the many by the few. The challenge that is already with us is the temptation to accept as true freedom what in reality is only a new form of slavery.'

'I have come to you as Bishop of Rome and Pastor of the whole Church, in order to celebrate this union with you in the sacrifice of the Eucharist, here in Ireland's capital city of Dublin, for the first time in Irish history. As I stand at this moment, a pilgrim for Christ to the land from which so many pilgrims for Christ, Peregrini Pro Christo, went out over Europe, the Americas, Australia, Africa, Asia, I am living a moment of intense emotion.'

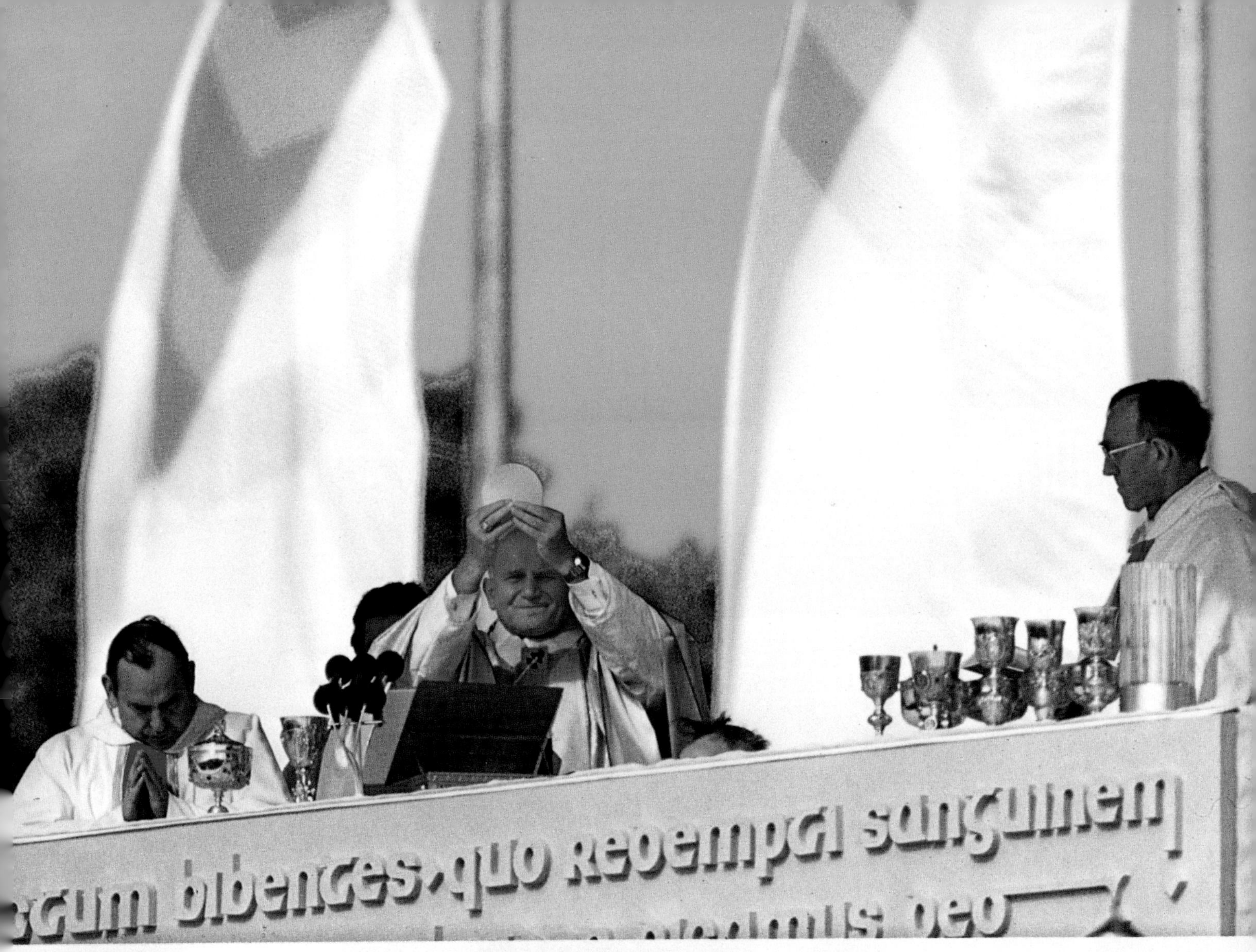

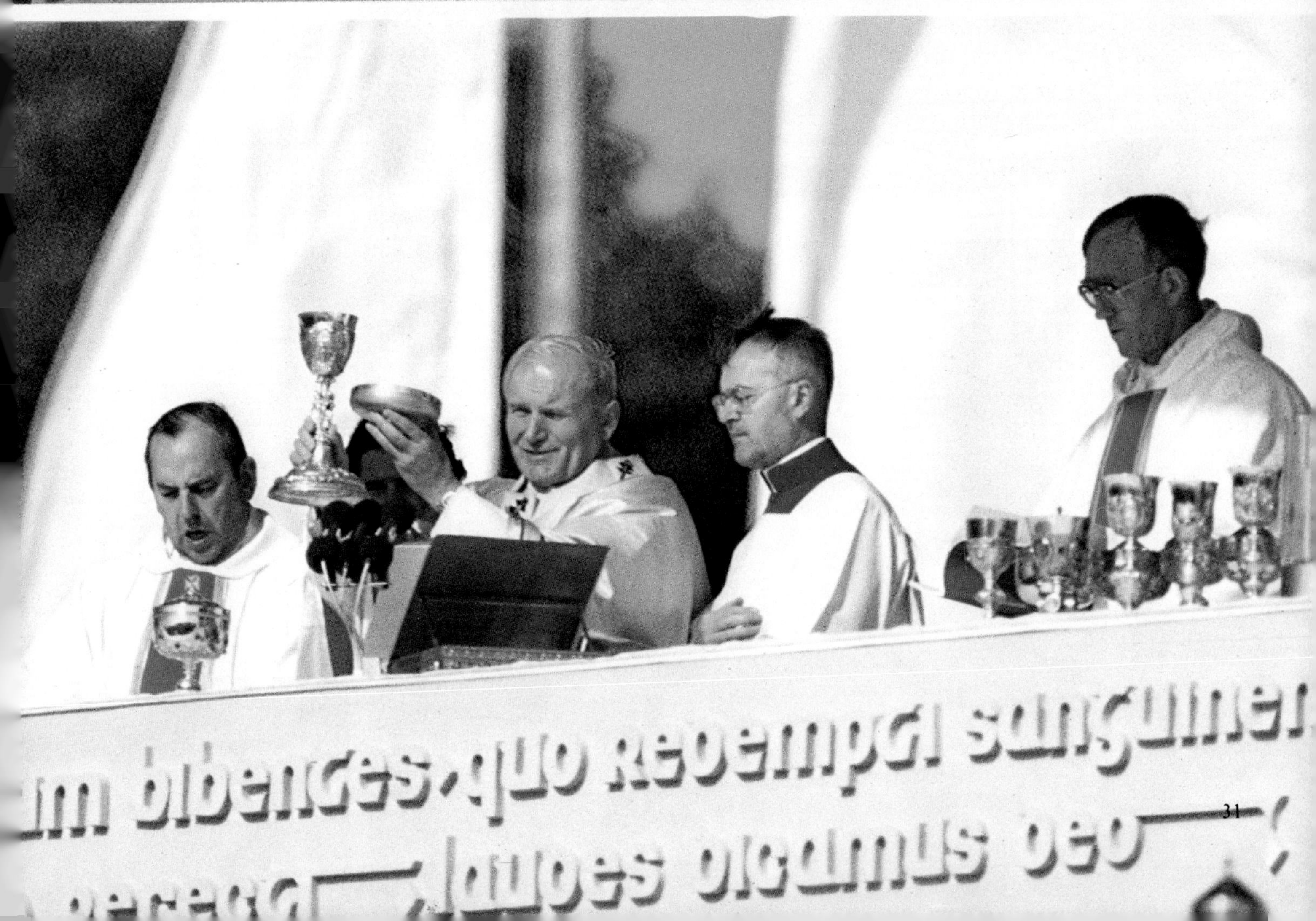

'And so, dear brothers and sisters, every act of reverence, every genuflection that you make before the Blessed Sacrament, is important because it is an act of faith in Christ, an act of love for Christ. And every Sign of the Cross and gesture of respect made each time you pass a Church is also an act of faith.'

'The truth of our union with Jesu
Christ in the Eucharist is teste
by whether or not we really lov
our fellow men and women; it i
tested by how we treat other
especially our families: husband
and wives, children and parent
brothers and sisters. It is teste
by whether or not we try to b
reconciled with our enemies, o
whether or not we forgive thos
who hurt us or offend us. It is teste
by whether we practise in life wha
our faith teaches us.'

THE POPE'S MESSAGE AT DROGHEDA

'Standing for the first time on Irish soil, on Armagh soil, the Successor of Peter cannot but recall the first coming here, more than 1,500 years ago, of Saint Patrick.

From his days as a shepherd boy at Slemish right up to his death at Saul, Patrick was a witness to Jesus Christ. Not far from this spot, on the Hill of Slane, it is said that he lit, for the first time in Ireland, the Paschal Fire so that the light of Christ might shine forth on all of Ireland and unite all of its people in the love of the one Jesus Christ.'

• • •

'Saint Oliver Plunkett, Primate of Ireland for 12 years, is for ever an outstanding example of the love of Christ for all men. As bishop, he preached a message of pardon and peace. He was, indeed, the defender of the oppressed and the advocate of justice, but he would never condone violence. For men of violence, his word was the word of the Apostle Peter: "Never pay back one wrong with another." As a martyr for the faith, he sealed by his death the same message of reconciliation that he had preached during his life. In his heart there was no rancour, for his strength was the love of Jesus, the love of the Good Shepherd who gives his life for his flock. His dying words were words of forgiveness for all his enemies.'

• • •

'The tragic events taking place in Northern Ireland do not have their source in the fact of belonging to different Churches and Confessions; that this is not – despite what is so often repeated before world opinion – a religious war, a struggle between Catholics and Protestants. On the contrary, Catholics and Protestants, as people who confess Christ, taking inspiration from their faith and the Gospel, are seeking to draw closer to one another in unity and peace. When they recall the greatest commandment of Christ, the commandment of love, they cannot behave otherwise.

But Christianity does not command us to close our eyes to difficult human problems. It does not permit us to neglect and refuse to see unjust social, or international situations. What

Christianity does forbid is to seek solutions to these situations by the ways of hatred, by the murdering of defenceless people, by the methods of terrorism. Let me say more: Christianity understands and recognises the noble and just struggle for justice; but Christianity is decisively opposed to fomenting hatred and to promoting or provoking violence or struggle for the sake of 'struggle'. The command, "Thou shalt not kill," must be binding on the conscience of humanity, if the terrible tragedy and destiny of Cain is not to be repeated.'

● ● ●

'Never before in the history of mankind has peace been so much talked about and so ardently desired as in our day.'

● ● ●

Peace is more and more clearly seen as the only way to justice; peace is itself the work of justice. And yet again, and again, one can see how peace is undermined and destroyed. Why is it then that our convictions do not always match our behaviour and our attitudes? Why is it that we do not seem to be able to banish all conflicts from our lives?'

'I proclaim, with the conviction of my faith in Christ and with an awareness of my mission, that violence is evil, that violence is unacceptable as a solution to problems, that violence is unworthy of man.

Violence is a lie, for it goes against the truth of our faith, the truth of our humanity. Violence destroys what it claims to defend: the dignity, the life, the freedom of human beings. Violence is a crime against humanity, for it destroys the very fabric of society. I pray with you that the moral sense and Christian conviction of Irish men and women may never become obscured and blunted by the lie of violence, that nobody may ever call murder by any other name than murder, that the spiral of violence may never be given the distinction of unavoidable logic or necessary retaliation. Let us remember that the word remains for ever: "All who take the sword will perish by the sword."'

● ● ●

'I appeal to all who listen to me; to all who are discouraged after the many years of strife, violence and alienation – that they attempt the seemingly impossible to put an end to the intolerable. I pay homage to the many efforts that have been made by countless men and women in Northern Ireland to walk the path of reconciliation and peace.

The courage, the patience, the indomitable hope for the men and women of peace have lighted up the darkness of these years of trial. The spirit of Christian forgiveness shown by so many who have suffered in their persons or through their loved ones have given inspiration to multitudes. In the years to come, when the words of hatred and the deeds of violence are forgotten, it is the words of love and the acts of peace and forgiveness which will be remembered. It is these which will inspire the generations to come.

To all of you who are listening I say: do not believe in violence; do not support violence. It is not the Christian way. It is not the way of the Catholic Church. Believe in peace and forgiveness and love; for they are of Christ.'

● ● ●

'Now I wish to speak to all men and women engaged in violence. I appeal to you, in language of passionate pleading. On my knees, I beg you to turn away from the paths of violence and to return to the ways of peace. You may claim to seek justice. I, too, believe in justice, and seek justice. But violence only delays the day of justice. Violence destroys the work of justice. Further violence in Ireland will only drag down to ruin the land you claim to love and the values you claim to cherish.

In the name of God I beg you: return to Christ, who died so that men might live in forgiveness and peace. He is waiting for you, longing for each one of you to come to him so that he may say to each of you: your sins are forgiven; go in peace.

I appeal to young people who may have become caught up in organisations engaged in violence, I say to you, with all the love I have for you, with all the trust I have in young people: do not listen to voices which speak the language of hatred, revenge, retaliation. Do not follow any leaders who

train you in the ways of inflicting death. Love life, respect life; in yourselves and in others. Give yourselves to the service of life, not the work of death.'

● ● ●

'My dear young people; if you have been caught up in the ways of violence, even if you have done deeds of violence, come back to Christ, whose parting gift to the world was peace. Only when you come back to Christ, will you find peace for your troubled consciences, and rest for your disturbed souls.

And, to you, fathers and mothers, I say: Teach your children how to forgive, make your homes places of love and forgiveness; make your streets and neighbourhoods centres of peace and reconciliation. It would be a crime against youth, and their future, to let even one child grow up with nothing but the experience of violence and hate.'

● ● ●

'To all who bear political responsibility for the affairs of Ireland, I want to speak with the same urgency and intensity with which I have spoken to the men of violence. Do not cause, or condone, or tolerate, conditions which give excuse, or pretext, to men of violence.

For those who resort to violence always claim that only violence brings about change. They claim that political action cannot achieve justice. You, politicians, must prove them to be wrong. You must show that there is a peaceful, political way to justice. You must show that peace achieves the works of justice, and violence does not.

I urge you who are called to the noble vocation of politics to have the courage to face up to your responsibility, to be leaders in the cause of peace, reconciliation and justice. If politicians do not decide and act for just change, then the field is left open to the men of violence. Violence thrives best when there is political vacuum and a refusal of political movement.'

● ● ●

'I came to Drogheda today on a great mission of peace and reconciliation. I come as a pilgrim of peace, Christ's peace. To Catholics, to Protestants, my message is peace and love. May no Irish Protestant think that the Pope is an enemy, a danger or a threat. My desire is that instead Protestants would see in me a friend and a brother in Christ. Do not lose trust that this visit of mine may be fruitful, that this voice of mine may be listened to. And, even if it were not listened to, let history record that at a difficult moment in the experience of the people of Ireland, the Bishop of Rome set foot in your land, that he was with you and prayed with you for peace and reconciliation, for the victory of justice and love over hatred and violence. Yes, this, our witness, finally becomes a prayer, a prayer from the heart for peace for the peoples who live on this earth, peace for all the people of Ireland.'

As the sun set, the Pope left Drogheda *above right* to return to Dublin where people thronged *right* to see his motorcade.

When the Pope met representatives of other churches, he told them:
'What a gift of God it is that there exists today among Christians a deeper realisation of need to be perfectly one in Christ and in His church.'

• • •

'Christians must unite together to promote justice and defend the rights and dignity of every human person.'

The Pope visited the sixth-century ruins of the monastery at Clonmacnoise, from where Irish monks once helped evangelise Europe. He then flew by helicopter to Galway to celebrate a special Mass for young people.

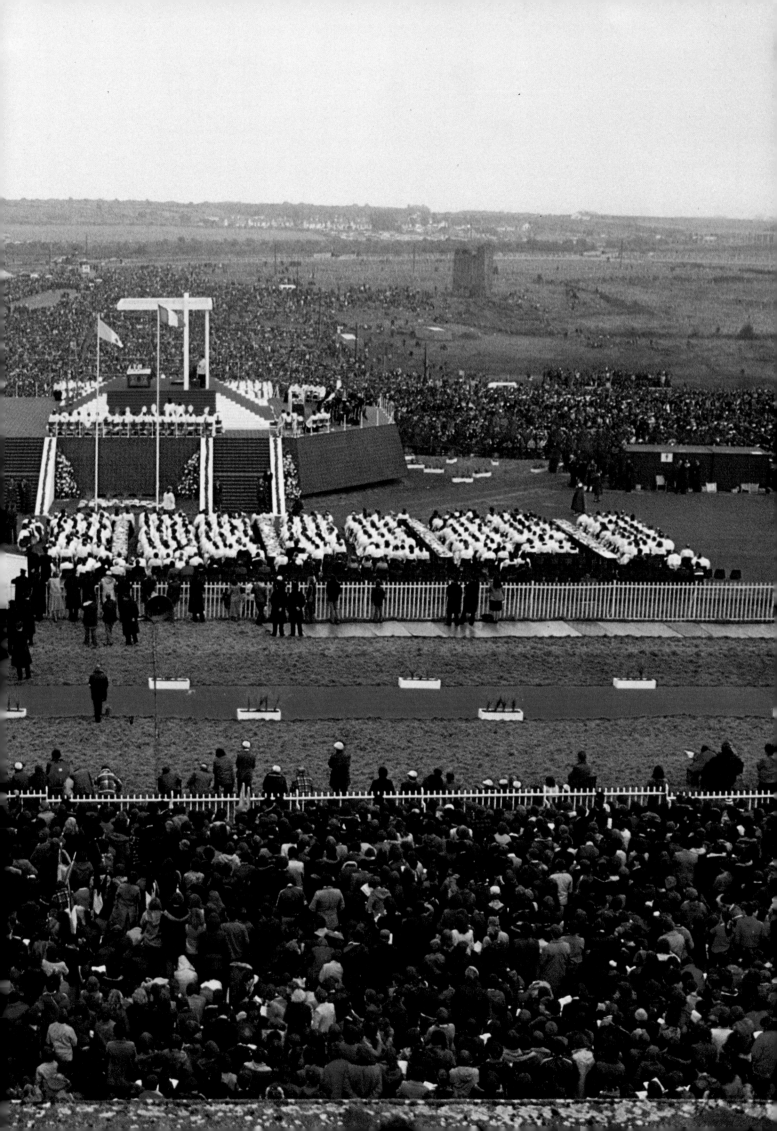

'I believe in youth, I believe in youth with all my heart, and with all the strength of my conviction. And today I say: I believe in the youth of Ireland! I believe in you who stand here before me, in every one of you.

When I look at you, I see the Ireland of the future. Tomorrow, you will be the living force of your country; you will decide what Ireland will be.'

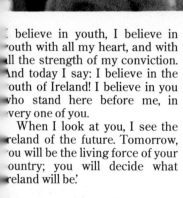

3

You will hear people tell you that your religious practices are hopelessly out of date, that they hamper your style and your future, that with everything that social and scientific progress has to offer, you will be able to organise your own lives, and that God has played out his role.'

• • •

'Yes, dear young people, do not close your eyes to the moral sickness that stalks your society today, and from which your youth alone will not protect you. How many young people have already warped their consciences and have substituted the true joy of life with drugs, sex, alcohol, vandalism and the empty pursuit of mere material possessions?

Something else is needed: something that you will find only in Christ, for he alone is the measure and the scale that you must use to evaluate your own life. In Christ, you will discover the true greatness of your own humanity.'

'Here I am at the goal of my journey to Ireland: the Shrine of Our Lady at Knock. Since I first learnt of the centenary of this Shrine, which is being celebrated this year, I have felt a strong desire to come here, the desire to make yet another pilgrimage to the Shrine of the Mother of Christ, the Mother of the Church, the Queen of Peace.'

• • •

'Today I am happy to be with the sick and the handicapped. I have come to give witness to Christ's love for you, and to tell you that the Church and the Pope love you too. They reverence and esteem you. They are convinced that there is something very special about your mission in the Church.'

'"Blessed are you among women, and blessed is the fruit of your womb!" These are the words with which Elizabeth, filled with the Holy Spirit, greeted Mary, her kinswoman from Nazareth.

"Blessed are you among women, and blessed is the fruit of your womb!" This is also my greeting to Muire Máthair Dé, Mary the Mother of God, Queen of Ireland, at this shrine of Knock. With these words I want to express the immense joy and gratitude that fills my heart today in this place. I could not have wanted it any differently. Highlights of my recent pastoral journeys have been the visits to the Shrines of Mary: to Our Lady of Guadalupe in Mexico, to the Black Madonna of Jasna Góra in my homeland, and three weeks ago to our Lady of Loreto in Italy. Today I come here because I want all of you to know that my devotion to Mary unites me, in a very special way, with the people of Ireland.'

58

All those who have come here have received blessings through the intercession of Mary. From that day of grace, the 21st of August, 1879, until this very day, the sick and suffering, people handicapped in body or mind, troubled in their faith or their conscience, all have been healed, comforted and confirmed in their faith because they trusted that the Mother of God would lead them to her son Jesus.

Every time a pilgrim comes up to what was once an obscure bogside village in Co.Mayo, every time a man, woman or child comes up to the Old Church with the Apparition Gable or to the new Shrine of Mary Queen of Ireland, it is to renew his or her faith in the salvation that comes through Jesus, who made us all children of God and heirs of the kingdom of heaven. By entrusting yourselves to Mary, you receive Christ.'

Joannes Paulus II P.

1. X. 79.

At the national seminary o
Maynooth *left* the Pope told those
who chose a religious vocation:
'You must work for the Lord with
a sense of urgency. You mus
work with the conviction that this
generation, this decade of the
1980s which we are about to enter
could be crucial and decisive for
the future of the faith in Ireland
Let there be no complacency'.

In his address at Limerick, before
his departure from Shannon
airport *right,* the Pope said:
'To all I say, revere and protec
your family and your family life
for the family is the primary field
of Christian action for the Irish
laity, the place where your "roya
priesthood" is chiefly exercised
The Christian family has been in
the past Ireland's greatest
spiritual resource'.

62

Slán agus Beannacht leat, Pápa Eóin Pól II

First published 1979 by Gill and Macmillan Ltd, 15/17 Eden Quay, Dublin 1,
with associated companies in London and Basingstoke, Delhi, Hong Kong,
Johannesburg, Lagos, Melbourne, New York, Singapore, Tokyo.
© 1979 Colour Library International Ltd./Irish Tourist Board.
Colour separations by FERCROM, Barcelona, Spain.
Display and text filmsetting by Focus Photoset, London, England.
Printed and bound by JISA-RIEUSSET, Barcelona, Spain.
All rights reserved. ISBN No. 7171 1028 1
GILL AND MACMILLAN LTD.